Bris 5/91

Asian Indians

by Susan gordon

DATE	ISSUED TO

Mills College Childrens School

Asian Indians

IMMIGRATION
AND THE
AMERICAN WAY OF LIFE

Geologically speaking, the continent of North America is very old. The people who live here, by comparison, are new arrivals. Even the first settlers, the American Indians who came here from Asia about 35,000 years ago, are fairly new, not to speak of the first European settlers who came by ship or the refugees who flew in yesterday. Whenever they came, they were all immigrants. How all these immigrants live together today to form one society has been compared to the making of a mosaic. A mosaic is a picture formed from many different pieces. Thus, in America, many groups of people—from African Americans or Albanians to Tibetans or Welsh—live side by side. This human mosaic was put together by the immigrants themselves, with courage, hard work, and luck. Each group of immigrants has its own history and its own reasons for coming to America. Immigrants from different regions have their own ways of creating communities for themselves and their children. In creating those communities, they not only keep elements of their own heritage alive, but also enrich further the fabric of American society. Each book in *Recent American Immigrants* will examine a part of this human mosaic up close. The books will look at some of the most recent arrivals to find out what they are like and how they fit into the whole mosaic.

Recent American Immigrants

ASIAN INDIANS

Susan Gordon

Consultant
Roger Daniels, Department of History
University of Cincinnati

Franklin Watts

New York • London • Toronto • Sydney

Developed by: Ω **Visual Education Corporation**
Princeton, NJ

Maps: Patricia R. Isaacs/Parrot Graphics

Cover Photograph: Bob Daemmrich/Stock Boston

Photo Credits: p. 3 (L) Tony Freeman/PhotoEdit; p. 3 (M) Bettina
Cirone/Photo Researchers, Inc.; p. 3 (R) Bill Anderson/Monkmeyer
Press Photo Service, Inc.; p. 11 North Wind Picture Archives;
p. 13 George D. Lepp/Comstock, Inc.; p. 17 Courtesy, Consulate
General of India; p. 19 Historical Pictures Service, Chicago;
p. 20 Margot Granitsas/The Image Works; p. 27 Bob Daemmrich/
The Image Works; p. 28 Robert Bruschini/Studio B; p. 30 Katrina
Thomas/Photo Researchers, Inc.; p. 33 Katrina Thomas/Photo
Researchers, Inc.; p. 35 Air-India Library; p. 36 Peter Menzel/Stock
Boston; p. 39 Stan Pantovic/Photo Researchers, Inc.; p. 41 Holt
Confer/The Image Works; p. 44 Cary Wolinsky/Stock Boston;
p. 46 Robert McElroy/Woodfin Camp & Associates; p. 48 Alain
Evrard/Photo Researchers, Inc.; p. 50 Masha Nordbye/Bruce
Coleman, Inc.; p. 53 (L) William Carter/Photo Researchers, Inc.;
p. 53 (R) Shelley Gazin/The Image Works; p. 54 Alon Reininger/
Woodfin Camp & Associates; p. 56 Peter Menzel/Stock Boston;
p. 57 In Stock/Photo Researchers, Inc.; p. 59 Kevin Horan/Stock
Boston; p. 61 Robert Brenner/PhotoEdit

Library of Congress Cataloging-in-Publication Data

Gordon, Susan, 1946-
Asian Indians/Susan Gordon.
p.   cm.— (Recent American immigrants)
Includes bibliographical references.
Summary: Discusses immigrants from India, their reasons for coming,
their lifestyles, and their contributions to their new country.
ISBN 0-531-10976-3
1. East Indian Americans — Juvenile literature. 2. United States —
Emigration and immigration — Juvenile literature. 3. India — Emigration and
immigration — Juvenile literature. [1. East Indian Americans.] I. Title.
II. Series: Recent American immigrants.
E184.E2G67   1990
973′.0491411 — dc20   90-12275 CIP AC

Contents

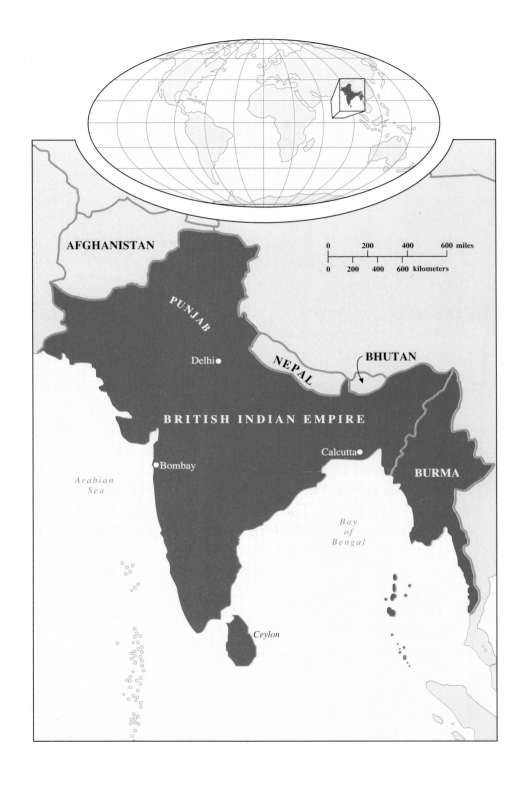

AFGHANISTAN

PUNJAB

Delhi●

NEPAL

BHUTAN

BRITISH INDIAN EMPIRE

●Bombay

Calcutta●

BURMA

Arabian
Sea

Bay
of
Bengal

Ceylon

0   200   400   600 miles

0   200   400   600 kilometers

The First and Second Waves, 1900–1965

Just after the turn of the century, the first wave of immigrants from India arrived in the United States. These few hundred men in turbans labored on the railroads and in the forests and fields of the West Coast. The wave of immigrants soon swelled as thousands more made the long journey from the other side of the world.

These first Asian Indians came as *sojourners*. That means that they planned on living in the United States only for a while. They intended to remain long enough to earn money to help their families and then return to India. Many did return. But many others stayed. They struggled with a new culture, a new language, and the mistrust on the part of Americans who did not understand their ways.

Their battle for acceptance went on for decades. When they arrived, American law barred them from becoming citizens.

New laws and regulations all but stopped their immigration by 1917. Some gave up and returned to India. Others waited hopefully for better times and a better place in American society. In the meantime, they found ways to survive as outsiders in an unfriendly land.

As the years passed, times and opinions changed, and so did immigration and citizenship laws. The long wait ended, and Asian Indians did become accepted as members of another ethnic group with the right to call the United States their home.

THE FIRST WAVE (1900–1946)

This table shows how many Asian Indians were living in the United States in four different years early in this century. The number went down over the years, because in 1917 Indians—along with other Asians—were barred from immigrating.

ASIAN INDIAN POPULATION IN THE UNITED STATES

1910	ca. 10,000
1920	ca. 15,000
1930	ca. 12,000
1940	ca. 10,000

Source: U.S. Census, Population Reference Bureau, and Roger Daniels.

Where Asian Indians Came From and Why   India is a large country in south central Asia. It is an ancient land, home of some of humankind's earliest civilizations. It is a diverse country, filled with people who speak almost 300 different languages and practice many different religions.

Nine out of every ten of the first immigrants came from the Punjab, a farming region in the north of India. They left India because land was growing scarce. Farmland was being divided into ever-smaller parcels as eldest sons inherited family farms. Younger sons, in response, became adventurers. Many were given the task of going to North America to earn money to help their families buy more land or pay debts. They were urged to go by their families. Most had never even traveled beyond their home villages before. Yet they were willing to go to a land thousands of miles away. They thought that they could earn more money in the United States than elsewhere.

Most of the young men immigrating from the Punjab were Sikhs. They followed a religion that required them to wear a turban at all times. That, and their dark skins, would set them apart once they arrived in North America. (You can read more about the Sikh religion on page 43.)

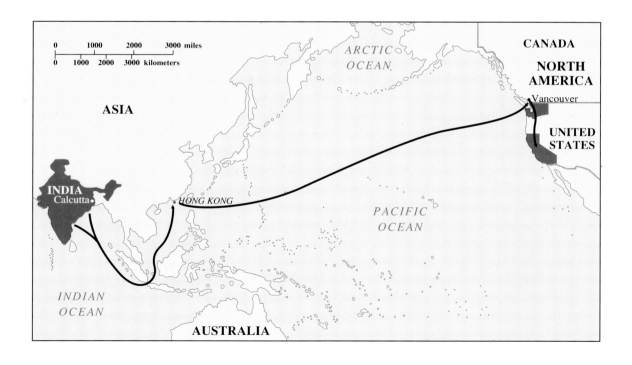

Where Asian Indians Landed   The trip from India was long. The immigrants had to travel first by train to Calcutta, then by ship to Hong Kong. No ships steamed directly from India to North America.

Hong Kong was the true departure point. There the immigrants left Asia and crossed the Pacific to land in Vancouver, on the West Coast of Canada. From that point the immigrants branched out to find work wherever they could.

WHERE ASIAN INDIANS WORKED

The American West in the early 1900s was a rich land that was just being developed. Workers were desperately needed to cut lumber, to build railroads, and to plant and harvest crops. Asian Indians helped supply that labor.

In the Forests   The sawmills and lumberyards of Washington were glad to hire Asian Indians, who would work long hours for low wages. White workers resented them for this, and trouble began. In 1907, hundreds of white workers in Bellingham, Washington, forced several hundred Asian Indians back into Canada. As town after town experienced such incidents, many immigrants headed south to California.

On the Railroads   In California, Asian Indians found jobs on the Western Pacific Railroad. From 1908 to 1910, thousands of these immigrants did heavy labor on the tracks. They repaired old track, and they also built hundreds of miles of new track. But as the job was finished, employment troubles began again. Unionized white workers worried that the few jobs available would be taken by Asian Indian immigrants, who were willing to work for lower wages. The union managed to bar Asian Indians from the railroad industry. Once again, Asian Indian immigrants were out of work. It was time to move on again. Many became laborers on California's farms.

An early view of a sawmill in Port Gamble, Washington.

On Farms In the early 1900s, farmers in the fertile valleys of California were desperate for help as they expanded their farms. For years, these farmers had hired Chinese and Japanese immigrants to work for them. But starting in 1882, a series of laws based on prejudice barred Chinese from immigrating to this country. As a result, there was a severe shortage of farm laborers in California. That made it easy for Asian Indians to get jobs. Because of their background, most were skilled at farming.

Traveling with the seasons, the new laborers went from farm to farm. They planted, cultivated, and picked fruits and vegetables. Much of this work was stoop labor, so called because the men had to work bent over or on their knees to perform tasks like cutting asparagus. They worked hard—up to fourteen hours a day. Still, the work paid far more than they would have earned in India. These earliest immigrants were soon joined by new arrivals coming directly from India.

LIFE IN CALIFORNIA

As farm laborers, the Asian Indians did contract work. That means they were hired only when work was needed, and they went from farm to farm. They lived in camps near the fields. "Home" might be a tent, a shed, or a barn. Living conditions were poor—the floor was often their only bed. And a dozen men might have to share that floor.

Besides fighting discrimination, the first wave of Asian Indians had to endure loneliness. Many were married but had left their families behind. Few women emigrated from India. During the years 1901 to 1910, only 109 of 5,800 Asian Indian immigrants were women. By relying on Punjabi traditions of leadership and cooperation, these men made the best of their situation.

Helping Each Other   Instead of traveling on their own, Asian Indian farm laborers organized themselves into groups of up to fifty men. Chosen as leader was the member who spoke the best English. He was in charge of finding work for the group. He also arranged for meals and shelter.

The members of each group shared each other's lives. Often they became as close as brothers. Shared meals provided members with companionship. Shared expenses helped them save money. If a group member died, the others paid for his funeral. They also sent money to the man's family in India.

Sharing meals provided more than companionship. Sharing also made it easier for the immigrants to eat the foods that their religions demanded. Sikhs ate mainly fruit, vegetables, milk, and butter. They also ate a flat bread called *roti* or *chapatis*. By cooking for themselves, the immigrants were able to prepare their native dishes.

Better Times   By the 1920s, a number of Asian Indians were able to save enough money to buy or lease their own farms. They rented or bought land from white landowners.

12

Asian Indians farmed much of the lush land in California's Sacramento Valley. This is a present-day aerial view of the valley with Mt. Shasta in the distance.

The Indian tradition of cooperation surfaced here, too. Men who had been in the same labor group often pooled their savings and became partners in farming. As many as eight men might work one farm. By 1920, Asian Indians were leasing more than 86,000 acres of rich California soil and owned more than 2,000 acres.

The new farmers worked even harder than they had as laborers. Eager for success, many worked nineteen-hour days. They grew traditional Indian crops, such as rice and cotton. But they also raised fruits, nuts, and vegetables.

Almost all the land owned or leased by the Asian Indians was located in just two areas—California's Imperial Valley and Sacramento Valley. They expected to be able to tend their crops in peace. Many hoped at last to send for their wives and families. Changes in laws, however, meant that neither of these plans could come true.

DISCRIMINATION AND THE LAW

Federal Law In 1917, Congress passed a law that prevented anyone from a large area of Asia from immigrating to the United States. India was included in this "barred zone." The law made it impossible for Asian Indians already here to be joined by their families. The law even banned married men from bringing their wives and children from India.

State Laws The California Alien Land Laws of 1913 and 1920 made life even more difficult for Asian Indians in this country. The law said that anyone who could not become a citizen could not own or even lease land. As a result, many Asian Indians were forced to give up their farms. Some became laborers again. Others decided to return to India. Still others found ways around the law. Those who had American-born children registered the land in the children's names. Because they were born in the United States, these children were citizens. Others had American friends, outraged by the law, buy or lease land in their own names.

Lonely, many Asian Indians wanted to start a family. But laws made it difficult. The 1917 law prevented Asian Indian women from coming. And in more than a dozen states, including California, Asian Indian men were forbidden to marry white women.

Many Asian Indian men married Mexican American women. Husbands and wives usually first met each other while working as farm laborers. Because they could become citizens, the wives could own or lease land. Many farms were soon registered under their names.

ASIAN INDIAN AND MEXICAN FAMILIES

In most marriages between Asian Indian men and Mexican women, the two different cultures blended. Usually, husband

and wife learned some of each other's language, but both kept their own religion. Because the mothers raised the children, the Mexican culture was carried on by the children.

Children   Children in these families, then, were more strongly influenced by Mexican culture than Asian Indian culture. Most of the children in these families had Spanish names. They spoke English and some Spanish, few could speak their father's language. Most were brought up as Catholics, with godparents from the mother's side, who helped raise them.

Many "Uncles"   In many households, children had several Indian "uncles" to help raise them. These "uncles" were not true family members, but old friends who had become their father's partners. Generous and kindly, the "uncles" treated the children as their own. Thus many children were brought up among Mexican American godparents and Sikh "uncles."

Family Problems   Blending cultures caused problems for many couples. Asian Indian men were not used to the fact that women in America enjoyed so much freedom. In India, married women were expected to obey their husbands at all times. They often had to get permission just to visit friends. Few Mexican American women were willing to live that way. They made their own decisions. Many wives refused, for example, to cook for the other men in the household. They also went shopping and visiting without asking permission from their husbands. Conflict often came out of these different ideas about marriage. As a result, at least two out of every ten of these mixed marriages ended in divorce.

But most couples learned to live with their differences. They created a kind of family life that blended their two cultures with American culture. They, like other such couples, were helping to form the American mosaic.

The Americanization of the Children   Children of these mixed marriages tended to leave their Indian heritage behind as they grew up. Because they worked many hours a day, seven days a week, Asian Indian fathers could not spend much time with their children. That made it difficult to give the children a sense of their Indian heritage.

As a result, few of the daughters allowed their fathers to arrange marriages with Indian men. (Arranged marriages were a common practice in India.) Those daughters who did enter an arranged marriage often got divorced. And because the number of possible partners was so limited, nine out of every ten children grew up and married outside the Asian Indian–Mexican American communities. These communities, which dotted the farming valleys of California, grew smaller and smaller as the children left their parents to start family life elsewhere. They were on their way to becoming part of the mainstream of American life.

OTHER COMMUNITIES

Sikh farmers from the Punjab were not the only Asian Indian immigrants who came to the United States in the early part of the century. Other, smaller groups came as well. Some were merchants or religious leaders. Some were students seeking an American education.

Merchants often went to New York and other cities in the East and Midwest. Students settled in university towns. Asian Indian students were an active group. During school vacations, a number of them worked as farm laborers. In this way they met the Punjabi farmers. They persuaded the farmers to provide college scholarships for needy students. Forbidden to join campus clubs, the students formed groups for themselves.

The Independence Movement   Most Asian Indian immigrants—including the Sikh farmers—became united in a

16

cause. Far from India, they worked to free their homeland from control by Great Britain, which had made India a colony in the nineteenth century. Students were often in the middle of that struggle.

To gather support for Indian independence, they formed patriotic groups. Most groups wanted independence to come about peacefully. They wanted to bring freedom to India by writing in newspapers and making speeches. In this way, they hoped to change people's minds. Many Indians went back to India to work for independence. One group in San Francisco tried to ship weapons to India.

India finally did gain independence from Great Britain in 1947. But it did not happen through the use of weapons. A leader named Mohandas K. Gandhi succeeded by using a policy of nonviolence.

Asian Indians, like members of many other ethnic groups, did not forget their homeland when they moved here. And America, its own freedom won through struggle, seemed a good place from which to work for independence.

The Indian flag was adopted shortly after independence was granted in 1947.

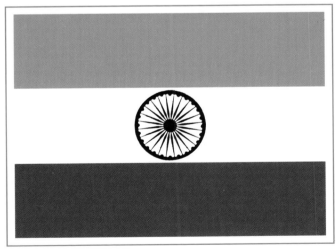

THE SECOND WAVE (1946–1965)

1946: Citizens at Last During the 1930s Asian Indians on the East Coast organized for another cause. This time, groups worked to convince the American government to change the laws that kept Asian Indians from becoming citizens. They were led by Sirdar Jagjit Singh, a Sikh merchant in New York City and president of the India League, one of those groups. They kept up their efforts for almost ten years.

In 1946, the government of the United States finally responded. Public Law 483, passed on July 2, 1946, gave Asian Indians the right to become naturalized citizens. These are people who gain citizenship by living in the United States for a certain number of years and pass a test. In addition, the law allowed 100 Asian Indians to enter the country each year. This was a very small number, but the law made another important change. It stated that once Asian Indians became citizens, they had the right to bring their husbands, wives, and children here. Many families were eventually reunited under the new law.

Public Law 483 granted entry to Asian Indian immigrants. But the flow—often called the second wave—remained a trickle. In the years from 1946 to 1965, slightly more than 6,000 Asian Indians came here. Then, in 1965, immigration laws opened the way for a greater number of immigrants.

ASIAN INDIAN POPULATION IN THE UNITED STATES

1950	ca. 14,000
1960	ca. 17,000
1965	ca. 20,000

Source: U.S. Census, Population Reference Bureau, and Roger Daniels.

Dalip Singh Saund

Once Asian Indians became eligible for citizenship, they gained another right. They became eligible for public office as well. Dalip Singh Saund, Congressman from California for three terms, was the first to benefit from that right. Dalip Singh Saund was born in 1899 to a wealthy family in the Punjab. His father, a contractor, could not read. He made sure, however, that his son could. Saund was sent to Punjab University, where he earned a degree in mathematics. After graduation, he went to California, where he entered the University of California at Berkeley. Saund quickly became a leader among Asian Indian students. Eventually he became president of a national student organization.

Saund was a scholar as well as a leader. He earned three advanced degrees, two in mathematics and one in agricultural science. Turning down job offers from two Indian universities, Saund became a rancher in California instead.

Saund and his wife, a Czech American, were well known in their community of Westmoreland in the Imperial Valley during the 1930s and 1940s. They did volunteer work for local causes. Saund also worked for Indian independence and for American citizenship for Asian Indians.

Public Law 483 enabled Saund to become a citizen, which he did in 1949. His community soon elected him a judge. He also became the Democratic candidate for Congress in 1956. When he won the election, Saund became the first Asian American to take a seat in Congress. Re-elected twice, Dalip Singh Saund served in Congress until 1963.

A street in Jackson Heights, Queens, an area in New York City where many Asian Indians live.

The Third Wave, 1965–1975

THE 1965 IMMIGRATION LAW

In 1965, a new law made sweeping changes in American immigration policy. This law did away with the old policy of a national quota system. With the quota system, only a certain number of immigrants were allowed from each country. With the new law, half the available immigrant spaces were to be filled with people from the Old World, and half with people from the New World. And as soon as immigrants became citizens, their immediate families could enter freely as permanent residents, bringing other extended family members. This new practice was called *chain migration*.

Once people from India were allowed to enter the United States in large numbers, they did. Now more than 500,000 Asian Indians live here. They are one of the fastest-growing ethnic groups in the United States.

Most of this third wave of immigrants is very different from the first group. That first wave was made up mainly of Sikh farmers from the Punjab. Now both men and women are coming from throughout India, and they are bringing their families with them. They are usually well educated and speak English fluently. Most are Hindu, but there are also Muslims, Sikhs, and members of other religious groups among them (pages 40–44 have more about India's religions).

As the pie charts show, immigrants from Asia are making up a larger and larger share of all immigrants to the United States. This greater share is a result of the 1965 Immigration Law.

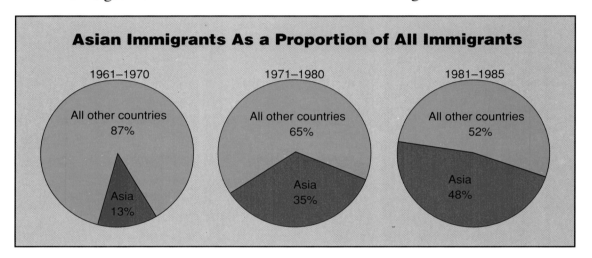

Asian Immigrants As a Proportion of All Immigrants

1961–1970
All other countries 87%
Asia 13%

1971–1980
All other countries 65%
Asia 35%

1981–1985
All other countries 52%
Asia 48%

The number of Asian Indians in the United States has grown dramatically since 1900. It should grow by about one-third again by the end of the century.

WHY ASIAN INDIANS COME

The great majority of these new Americans still come for economic reasons. India is a poor country that cannot supply enough jobs for its educated people. In 1970, for example, 20,000 doctors were out of work in India. In 1974, 100,000 engineers could not find jobs.

Salaries are another problem in India, where even highly trained workers are poorly paid. In the United States doctors can earn at least fifteen times what they would in India. Such differences in income make the United States very attractive.

The new immigrants are also attracted to the United States by the success of friends and family members who came before them. Visits and letters help convince them that they, too, can find better opportunities in the United States. Many of the immigrants come because they feel disappointed in India, a country that educates more people than it can employ.

A number of Asian Indians come originally to improve their opportunities back in India. They plan to attend college in the United States and then return to their homeland. Indians who receive American educations are paid much higher salaries than those educated in India. But many who come as students decide to remain as citizens.

ASIAN INDIAN POPULATION IN THE UNITED STATES

Year		Population
1970	ca.	75,500
1980	ca.	387,000
1990 (est.)	ca.	684,000
2000 (est.)	ca.	1,000,000

Source: U.S. Census, Population Reference Bureau, and Roger Daniels.

Better Opportunities For most Asian Indian immigrants, the United States offers the opportunities they hoped for. And Asian Indians have been very successful. They earned an average of $18,707 each in 1979. That makes them the highest income group among the recent immigrants in the United States. From earning little in India, they have moved up to having a comfortable living in the United States.

EDUCATION

The Asian Indians in this country are an extremely well educated group of people. The 1980 census reports that more than 93 percent of the men and almost 88 percent of the women are high school graduates. More than half are also college graduates, and many have advanced degrees. Among young adults of ages 20 to 24, more than 44 percent were enrolled in colleges and universities. This emphasis on education continues among the younger generation.

The Brain Drain   Each year a large number of India's educated people emigrate to the United States. Many Indian doctors, for example, leave the country after training. And many who come to the United States for professional training decide to remain once their student days are over. This outward flow of the highly trained people is a great loss to India in a number of ways. The popular phrase "brain drain" describes this loss and is easy to remember.

The Indian government invests many thousands of dollars in educating its professional and technical workers. In a sense, the country invests in its future by doing so. When these people leave, India loses that investment. According to one estimate, the cost of educating the 3,062 scientists, engineers, and doctors who migrated to the United States in just one five-year period (1962–1967) was $61,240,000. The United States is now benefiting from the education India provided for these people.

Some people think it is not fair to hire immigrant professionals. Then young people trained here will not find jobs. Clearly, however, we benefit from receiving more trained workers.

India is not alone in the problem of brain drain. Many other Third World countries cannot supply work for their college graduates. They also lose skilled workers to the United States.

OCCUPATIONS

The Asian Indians in this country hold many different kinds of jobs. They are accountants, computer scientists, lawyers, hairdressers, sales representatives, and managers. And, as in the past, some are farmers or work at other manual jobs.

Most Asian Indians in professions such as law and medicine find jobs in their chosen field. About 25,000 Asian Indian doctors and dentists now practice here, as well as 40,000 engineers. In fact, the percentage of Asian Indians who are professionals and managers is the highest of any Asian American group (see the graph on page 26).

For Asian Indians with less training, the story is somewhat different. Most in the field of health care do find jobs for which they have been trained, but large numbers are not able to exercise the skills they have. They do, however, find work in other fields. The level of unemployment among Asian Indians is very low.

Thousands of Asian Indians start their own businesses. Some of these entrepreneurs serve the local Asian Indian community by opening Indian grocery stores. Others start travel or insurance agencies, dry cleaning shops, or car rental agencies. Newspaper stands and stationery stores are also popular business ventures. Still others run restaurants that specialize in Indian foods, while a number own shops that sell clothes from India. By importing Indian products, they are helping the Indian economy as well as themselves. They are also helping us learn about another culture.

Asian Indians have been especially successful in the hotel business. They now own thousands of motels and hotels throughout the country. Sometimes, college-educated owners let their wives and children run the business while they themselves work in their professions.

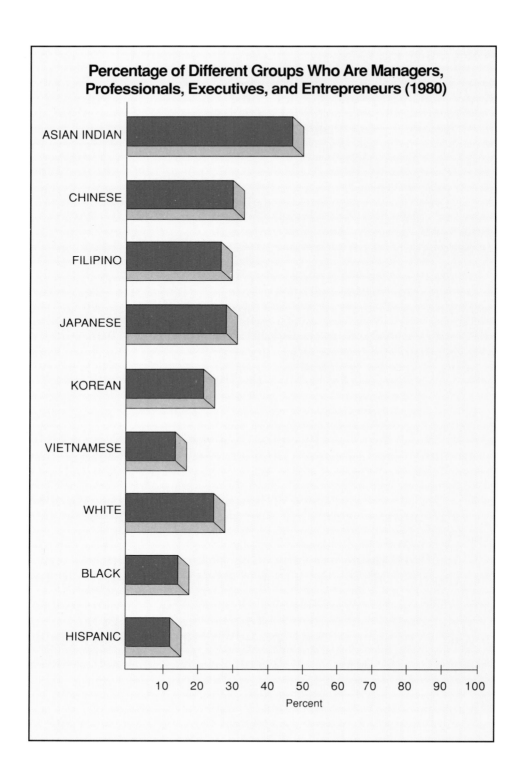

Women   About the same number of Asian Indian women as men now immigrate to the United States. Many come with their husbands, while others come on their own. Usually, Asian Indian women have had less opportunity for higher education than men. Still, many are well educated and hold professional positions. More than half of all Asian Indian women in this country work outside the home, although compared with other Asian groups, their figure is low. Almost half of these women hold professional positions. They, too, are doctors and dentists, engineers and lawyers.

Asian Indian women living in the United States have far more freedom in their job choices than they would in India. In India, only about 13 percent of women work outside the home. Here, Asian Indian women not only work, but they also hold positions of great responsibility. A large number of these working women, for example, own or manage shops. In India, in contrast, men usually run shops.

Since passage of the 1965 Immigration Act, many Asian Indian women have come to the United States. A large number are doctors and other professionals.

Sandhya Dholakia

"Coming here wasn't an easy decision, because we are both thirty-five now, and we have a ten-year-old son. We applied for immigration eight years ago in 1981, and we got the visa in 1987. When we finally got the call, we wondered if we should go, but we knew deep inside we would go. We wanted to give our child a better quality of life than we would be able to do in India. We wanted him to be able to go to college in the United States.

"We also wanted to give ourselves a better quality of life than is available to even the upper middle class in India. My husband was earning a very good salary working for a bank, and I was a professor of economics in a college. Even so, there was no way that we could ever have saved enough to buy a house and a car.

"We didn't know what would happen when we came here. Even though I had no problem speaking English, I had a lack of confidence. One of the few things we bought was a television. I spent two months watching television so I could speak English the way people do here. Then I was able to get a job with a bank as a market research analyst.

"We're very savings-oriented because we are so insecure about the future. The main reason we've come here is to give our child the best education possible. I want to be sure that I never have to tell our son that he can't go to college because we don't have the money.

"We saved for a year and put a down payment on a condominium. We hardly spent money on anything. We didn't eat out at all. I haven't seen a single movie since I came to the United States because these are things I feel I can do without so we can go for the big things. I came here, I set my goals, and I will move toward them.

"At work in India I always wore the traditional sari, and I miss it so. I haven't worn a single sari since I came here. I had about eighty of them, but I didn't bring any because I had to pack a whole household into four suitcases. I wear Western clothes now because it's easier, even at home.

"I have seen my friends make a point of having Indian dinners, but we are not fussy about food. For the first couple of years we ate more Western food, but now I'm beginning to miss the kind of food we had at home. The only way to get it is to make it myself, so I've started cooking more often. But our son loves hamburgers and pizza.

"We have seen a lot of our friends work hard to make sure their children remain Indian. With us it's the other way around. While our son should know where he comes from, we have consciously planned that he is going to be brought up as an American. We don't want to create a dilemma between how to behave at home because we're Indian, and how to behave outside.

"I have a lot of good friends here now, both American and Indian. Americans have been incredibly supportive. When people at work found out we didn't have furniture, they gave me furniture. I can't believe it. Even emotionally, they've said, 'We're here for you. You don't have to worry that you have your family so far away.' America is a very friendly country, and it's very accepting. I know we've come to the right place. I feel that we've come home."

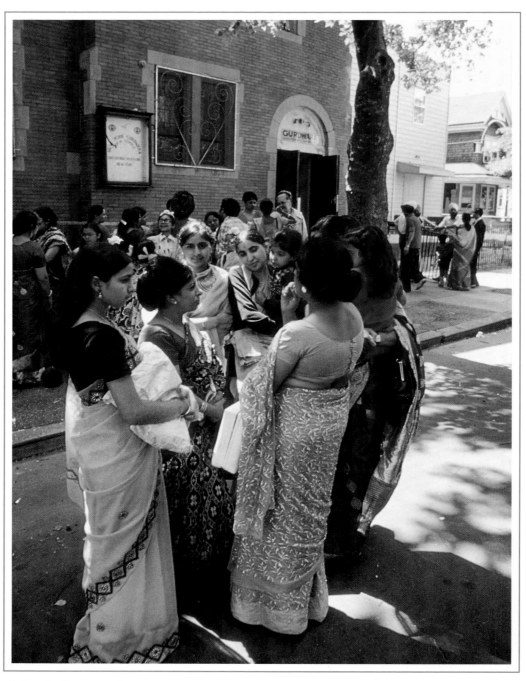

Asian Indians socializing outside the Gurdwara Temple (Sikh), Queens, New York.

WHERE ASIAN INDIANS LIVE

Like other people, Asian Indians often live where they find work. For professionals, that usually means in and near cities. Many Asian Indian doctors live in or near cities in the Northeast and Midwest. New York City boasts an Asian Indian community of more than 40,000. Chicago, Illinois, which comes in second, is home to more than 23,000 Asian Indians. (At one time, almost half the doctors in one large Chicago hospital were Asian Indians.) Engineers and other scientists often go to the area near San Francisco and to Houston. Their skills are in demand there. Smaller Asian Indian communities are located in college towns throughout the country.

A warm climate has a special attraction for Asian Indians, who come from a hot, sunny land. That is one reason more than 57,000 Asian Indians live in California. Surprisingly, though, almost none live in Hawaii.

As with other immigrant groups, most Asian Indian communities grow larger as relatives and friends also immigrate to the United States. The newcomers want to live near the people they know and love.

STATES WITH THE LARGEST ASIAN INDIAN POPULATION, 1980 (Total U.S. Asian Indian Population, 387,000)	
New York	68,000
California	60,000
Illinois	37,000
New Jersey	31,000
Texas	23,000
Pennsylvania	17,000
	236,000

Source: U.S. Census

TWO ASIAN INDIAN COMMUNITIES

California Farms   By 1965, the Asian Indian farm communities that had grown up in the Sacramento Valley had dwindled in numbers. Many of the original farm workers had moved away after World War II. Others had returned to India. But the third wave of immigration quickly brought new life to these aging farm communities. Now that they were citizens, community members began to sponsor other family members, who often lived with them and helped work their farms.

Attracted by the existence of a growing Punjabi community, thousands more Sikh immigrants moved into the area during the 1970s. Many of these immigrants later moved to the cities of California to find jobs in business or the professions. But others stayed to continue the Sikh tradition of farming. Within a few years, Sikh-owned farms covered more than 7,000 acres in the area. Hundreds of Sikh families also now cultivate crops near Fresno.

Asian Indians in New York   With a population of more than 40,000 Asian Indians, New York City has an especially rich Indian culture. Lined with Indian restaurants and shops selling Indian spices, foods, clothing, and jewelry, one area is even known as "Little India."

The storeowners are often relatives of professionals who came earlier. They work hard and are making successes of their businesses. Some longtime storeowners in the city are even beginning to complain about competition. Others are glad to have Asian Indians rent empty store space.

The Asian Indian community in New York City can listen to Indian radio stations, go to Indian movie theaters, and visit temples of the major Indian religions. Dozens of associations promoting Indian culture are also located in the city. Each summer they sponsor an Indian festival in Central Park that is attended by thousands of people of all ethnic backgrounds.

MARRIAGE AND FAMILY LIFE

Most Asian Indians are already married when they come here. Marriage and family are greatly valued in India, where families live close to their relatives. Several generations may live under the same roof.

Asian Indians in this country work hard to maintain traditional family values. Divorce among Asian Indians is almost as rare here as it is in India. More than 90 percent of Asian Indian couples in this country stay married.

Many Asian Indians in the United States follow traditions for special occasions, such as this Hindu wedding.

During the 1960s and 1970s, new immigrants from India usually lived in families made up of two parents and their children. For women who stayed at home, that often meant a lonely life. They missed nearby relatives to count on for advice and companionship. Now that picture is changing. Almost half of the immigrants who have come here since 1975 live in homes that may also include an aunt, an uncle, or a grandparent. These relatives can help pass on Indian heritage to the children in the household.

Some things change greatly for Asian Indian families once they start life here. In India, only about 13 percent of women work outside the home. In contrast, more than half the Asian Indian women in this country work. That can mean great changes in family life.

Going Home to Be Married   One tradition that remains active among Asian Indian immigrants is the arranged marriage. In such a marriage, parents choose a young person's bride or groom. Even when they have been here for some time, immigrants who are single return to India for an arranged marriage. Parents may also arrange marriages for children who have been born and raised here. They, too, may go to India for their wedding.

Maintaining Ties   Like all immigrant groups, Asian Indians want two things for themselves and their children: They want to be accepted as Americans and adapt to American ways. And they want to preserve and pass along their culture and heritage.

Asian Indians in this country do a lot to maintain ties with their homeland. They write to their families frequently and call as often as possible. Most also try to visit India every few years. Families with children consider these visits especially important. Parents want their children to experience Indian culture firsthand and spend time with their Indian relatives and

34

friends. During school vacations, older children may be sent on their own to visit relatives.

Frequent visits are made in the other direction, too. Most families are happy to host friends and family members from India. Long visits are an Indian tradition, and visitors may stay for months. When these visitors are older relatives, they usually help teach children Indian customs.

Family visits from India help Asian Indians in America maintain cultural ties.

Asian Indians in the United States Today

Another way to maintain ties with family members is to bring them to live permanently in the United States. That is exactly what thousands of Asian Indian immigrants do and have done since 1946. The law allows naturalized citizens to sponsor relatives. Just one person may sponsor dozens of family members. One businessman in Ohio began a long chain by sponsoring the immediate members of his family. They sponsored other relatives, including those by marriage. As a result, this Ohio man has indirectly sponsored the immigration of 82 members of his extended family!

In time, these immigrants become naturalized citizens themselves. Then they, too, can sponsor relatives. Often these newest immigrants live at first with family members who have come here before them. As this chain immigration continues, entire families may leave India for the United States.

A Different Group   Chain immigration is bringing in a new and different wave of Asian Indians. Often these are people who would not think of immigrating on their own. They may not speak English well when they arrive. They count on family members who are familiar with the United States. Unlike the third wave, with its many professionals, these immigrants have far less education. They may, for example, be farm or factory workers. Often they are paid below the minimum wage by employers who take advantage of them. Yet, as they themselves state, they are better off than they would be in India, where the average yearly income is $100.

These immigrants can move up in the world. A number have opened their own businesses. Others work long hours for relatives who own such businesses, hoping for the day when they themselves can do the same. Asian Indians now tend most of the thousands of subway newsstands in New York City.

LIFE IN THE UNITED STATES

Immigrants from any country adopt some American ways. The same is true of Asian Indians. Both parents and children in Asian Indian families are influenced by American life. Many Asian Indians, for example, wear Western-style dress. Like all immigrant groups, Asian Indians also try to maintain their own culture.

At work and in school, Asian Indians are part of the mainstream of American life. At home, though, they express the Indian part of themselves.

Changing Roles   With so many women working, traditional Indian family patterns of life have changed in the United States. Men have started to step in and help with home and family. Women, though, almost always prepare the meals, especially the evening meal. That meal is the focus of family life in most Asian Indian homes.

Language   In many homes, English is the usual language, as it often was in India. Owing to the long British rule in India, English was the official government language and was—and is—learned by many Indians in school. Many newspapers were also published in English. The language became the main way to communicate and a unifying force among Indians who, among themselves, spoke many different languages. In some homes, husbands and wives speak to each other in their native Indian language. Often they speak to their children in that language, too. The children, especially those born in this country, may answer in English.

Child Rearing   Children, in particular, feel American influences. They go to American schools and play American games and sports. They also watch American television, often for many hours a week. The effects of television have shocked some parents into teaching their children more about India. These parents discovered that their children knew far more about American cartoon heroes than about gods in Indian religions.

This young father and his daughter are part of one of the oldest American Sikh communities in Yuba City, California.

Asian Indian parents are usually worried about their children adopting some American ways. To keep that from happening, parents do their best to bring up children in traditional ways. In some Indian homes, a grandparent helps teach the children Indian language, religion, and customs. Many parents have also started showing children Indian films. Some children attend Indian language and culture classes.

Like the children of many other immigrant groups, Asian Indian children may end up feeling that they are part of two cultures. They may feel themselves to be Indian in some situations and American in others.

RELIGIOUS LIFE IN AMERICA

Religion is one area in which Asian Indians maintain their ways. By practicing their religions, they keep their sense of themselves as Indians. Many immigrants, in fact, have become even more religious since coming to the United States. They are careful to teach their children about their rich religious heritage. India is the home of some of the most ancient religions in the world.

Hindus   The great majority of Indians (some 500 million) are Hindus. Hinduism is both a religion and a way of life. The basic beliefs of Hinduism, as well as rules for daily life, are set down in the Vedas. These holy books were written about 2,500 years ago. Among the basic ideas is the belief that all living creatures share in one universal spirit. As a result, Hindus are vegetarians. They believe that no animal should be harmed, since they, too, have souls. Cows, in fact, are sacred to Hindus and are often allowed to roam free.

Hindus also believe in rebirth, or reincarnation. Their religion teaches that when people die, they are born again as another living creature, such as a cat or a horse or a person. A person's actions determine what kind of creature he or she

40

becomes. Someone who has been evil, for example, may be reborn as an insect. Every action, even the smallest one, affects a person's next life.

Hindus worship many gods and goddesses. Each one is a different aspect of a universal god. To worship, Hindus often go to a temple. But many Hindu ceremonies, including weddings, take place at home. In larger homes, a room is set aside especially for worship.

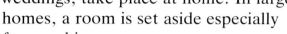
This Hindu temple was built in Malibu, California so that Asian Indians could worship following ancient customs.

Castes   For five centuries, Hindus have followed a special class system. The Vedas divided all Hindus into four main groups called *castes*. Each caste, and its many subcastes, has a traditional occupation. Priests and scholars make up the highest caste. Servants and laborers make up the lowest one. Each caste has special rules for diet and behavior. In the past, the castes did not mix with each other. Modern life, however, has broken down some of the barriers, especially among Asian Indians who have come to the United States. Many parents, for example, do not object if their children want to marry outside their caste. Most Indians in the United States are either of the higher castes or are Sikhs, who do not believe in the caste system.

Hindu Culture in America   Hindu communities in this country express their Hinduism in a variety of ways. Through active fund-raising, they have built more than 100 temples in different parts of the country. To build just one Hindu temple may require contributions totaling several hundred thousands of dollars.

Hindu temples are a focus for the Asian Indian community. They hold Sunday services, as well as a variety of activities each week. These may attract people from miles away, giving Asian Indians a chance to enlarge their circle of friends in the community.

Most Hindus belong to at least one local or national Hindu organization. These groups send out newsletters and sponsor speakers, artists, and missionaries. They also have gatherings for the local Hindu community.

To teach their children about Hinduism, most parents make a point of taking them to religious festivals. They also buy special children's books about Hinduism when they visit India. Some communities have Sunday schools, much like those of other religions. Almost every home has a special place reserved for worship.

Muslims   Five of every hundred people in India are Muslim—followers of Islam. Islam is related to both Judaism and Christianity, especially in its belief in one God. It was begun 1,300 years ago by the prophet Mohammed.

When India became independent in 1947, the majority of Muslims split away and formed their own country, called Pakistan. Later, a large number of Muslims formed a third country, called Bangladesh.

Muslim laws regarding worship and behavior come from the Muslim holy book, the Koran, and from the rules taught by Mohammed. Muslims must pray five times a day. In addition, they must go to a Muslim temple, called a *mosque,* for services every Friday. Muslims may not eat pork or drink alcohol. As a special act of faith, they must make a pilgrimage to Mecca if possible at least once before they die.

Muslims make up a very small part of the Asian Indian community in this country. For that reason, it has been important for them to organize. They have built mosques and started associations to keep their faith active.

Sikhs   The Sikh religion was founded more than 400 years ago by Guru Nanak. His goal was to combine Hinduism and Islam. He did away with the Hindu caste system but kept the belief in rebirth. Like the Muslims, he taught that there was one God.

Like Hindus and Muslims, Sikhs must follow certain rules. Men must not cut their hair, which they wear knotted under a turban. Sikhs may not drink alcohol or smoke.

The Sikhs in this country live mainly in California, where they make up more than 30 percent of the Asian Indian population. A number of Sikh temples serve the community.

Other Religions   Small groups of Asian Indian immigrants here practice two other ancient religions—Jainism and Zoroastrianism.

Jains Most of the Jains in India live in the western part of the country. Founded more than 2,500 years ago, Jainism is one of the gentlest religions in the world. The basic belief of Jains is that no living creature should be harmed. To that end, they sweep the path in front of them to be sure they do not step on any living creatures. Jains do not eat meat. They also avoid root vegetables because pulling them up may harm worms and insects.

Zoroastrians Founded some 2,700 years ago by a prophet named Zoroaster in ancient Persia, Zoroastrianism teaches belief in one God. In that respect, the religion resembles the Jewish, Christian, and Muslim faiths. Zoroastrians also believe that the world is divided into forces of good and evil. It is up to people to choose the good side. They can do this through good thoughts, good words, and good deeds.

In India, followers of this religion belong to the Parsi sect. About 120,000 Parsis live in Bombay, where they settled when they fled Persia to find religious freedom.

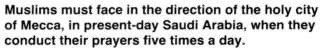

Muslims must face in the direction of the holy city of Mecca, in present-day Saudi Arabia, when they conduct their prayers five times a day.

KEEPING INDIAN CULTURE ALIVE

Besides practicing their religions, Indians in this country have found other ways to keep their culture alive. They form regional schools to teach Indian language, music, and dance to people in their communities. They publish newspapers about Indian life. They show Indian films and sponsor Indian performers. They also put on colorful festivals to celebrate Indian holidays. Non-Indians are welcome at many of these events, which seek to educate Westerners as well as to entertain Indians.

Forming Groups   Hundreds of local and several national associations help Indian communities hold on to their heritage. Local associations usually bring together people from one region in India who speak the same language. Many meetings take place on a weekend and last an entire day. This is the time for members to share their Indian heritage and pass it on to their children. The program, conducted in their native tongue, may include songs, a play, or a movie. A high point of the day is a feast of regional dishes. People often share the labor to prepare all the food. They may also share their homes with other Indians who have to drive long distances in order to attend the festival.

National associations have somewhat different goals. They seek to bring together Indians from many regions. One group, the Indian Festival Committee, unites different groups for the annual India Festival Day in New York City. This famous festival celebrates many varieties of Indian music, dance, clothing, and food.

One national group, the Association of Indians in America (AIA) has political as well as cultural goals. In 1977, the AIA persuaded the federal government to declare Asian Indians as a separate ethnic group starting in 1980. In this way, Asian Indians hope to establish a clearer identity for themselves.

Zubin Mehta

One of the great conductors of classical music, Zubin Mehta was born in 1936 to a Parsi family in Bombay, India. The Parsis had fled Persia in the eighth century to seek religious freedom. They settled in Bombay, where many became well-to-do and well educated. During the 1930s, the Parsis heard Western classical music for the first time and made it their own.

Zubin Mehta's father, Mehti Mehta, was a violinist and conductor. He began teaching Zubin to play the violin and piano when the boy was just seven. By his teens, Zubin was conducting the orchestra during rehearsals.

Zubin was clearly a musical wonder. But his mother convinced him to study medicine, which he did for two years. Then, when he was eighteen, he realized that he was meant to be a musician. He went to Vienna, considered to be the capital of classical music. Mehta entered the Vienna Academy to study conducting and composing. He also learned the double bass. He quickly became good enough to play with the Vienna Chamber Orchestra. In 1957, Mehta graduated from the Academy with a degree in conducting. His career immediately took off.

Along with one hundred other contestants, Mehta went to England in 1958 to enter a conductors' competition. He took first place and won a one-year contract as associate director of the Royal Liverpool Philharmonic Orchestra.

When his contract ended, Mehta began to tour the world as a guest conductor. During the next few years, he conducted symphony orchestras in Vienna, Montreal, New York City, and Los Angeles.

Mehta was so successful that in 1961 he was named conductor of the Los Angeles Philharmonic. He and his family settled in that city. A year later, he was named conductor of the Montreal Symphony. With those appointments, Mehta achieved two firsts. He was the youngest person to become conductor of a major orchestra in the United States. He was also the first person to be the conductor of two major orchestras during the same period. Mehta did well with this unusual joint appointment, which required a great amount of work and travel. Both orchestras flowered under his direction.

Mehta has since worked with many more orchestras. He became adviser to the Israel Philharmonic in 1969, and was named musical director for life twelve years later. In 1978, Mehta became director of the New York Philharmonic, which he led until 1989. He has also conducted operas in some of the great opera houses of the world.

His amazingly busy schedule has also included regular appearances as guest conductor with other orchestras. In addition, he has made many recordings with various orchestras. India has recognized Mehta's contributions to the world of classical music by giving him their highest cultural award, the Order of the Lotus.

An array of spicy Asian Indian dishes.

FOOD IN INDIA AND AMERICA

The people of India eat a great variety of food. People's diets are set by three things—the foods they can raise, the region they live in, and the religion they practice.

Most Indians are vegetarians. Throughout India, food is highly spiced, especially the curries, which are rich stews made with vegetables and meat, fish, or eggs. And throughout India, food is the basis of hospitality.

The Staples Certain kinds of foods appear at meals in all kinds of Indian homes. A flat, unleavened bread called *chapati* is served where wheat is the main grain. In other areas, flat breads are made with rice. Vegetarians get their protein from beans and dairy products. Meat eaters make dishes with lamb, chicken, beef, or fish.

Dairy products are important in Indian cooking. Many well-known dishes are made with yogurt. These cool, refreshing dishes are used to set off the spicier foods during a meal.

A great variety of fresh fruits and vegetables are also used. Spinach and mustard greens are popular vegetables, as are eggplant, cabbage, turnips, okra, cucumbers, and potatoes. Mangoes are the most popular fruit, along with lemons and oranges. Asian Indians also enjoy papayas, melons, breadfruit, guavas, pomegranates, and tamarinds, among others.

In India, tea is drunk all day long.

Eating in the United States Asian Indians here can get the ingredients for their native dishes from Indian grocery stores. Muslims, who eat no pork, often buy kosher foods. Many former vegetarians, however, now eat meat.

Most Asian Indians in this country eat American as well as Indian foods, but usually not at the same meal. Breakfast and lunch are often American-style. Dinner, however, is usually Indian-style. Children are most likely to eat American foods, especially fast foods.

Cooking the Indian Way

In a kitchen in India, food preparation goes on all day. In middle-class homes in India, much of it is done by servants. Almost all foods are purchased raw and treated at home. Indians grind and roast their own grains and coffee. They make their own mixtures of spices. They preserve their own fruits and vegetables. And they bake their own bread, often over a charcoal stove shaped like a bucket.

The tools used in an Indian kitchen are very different from those used here. There are coconut scrapers and marrow spoons, as well as special tools for twisting dough into spaghetti-like shapes. Even a basic vegetable peeler is different. In India, the peeler is fixed to a board so that the cook moves the vegetable, not the peeler. With these simple tools, Indian cooks turn out elegant meals.

A spice market in India.

In the United States, many people have become interested in Indian foods. Here is a tasty curry recipe, made simple for the American cook. It is a good recipe for using up leftovers, though fresh lamb or chicken may also be used. In India, the curry powder itself would be made from several fresh spices such as coriander, ginger, cinnamon, cloves, and cardamom. Read the recipe through before begining to cook.

A sharp knife must be used to prepare the onions, garlic, and meat, so an adult should stand by to help. Always use potholders with a hot pan.

Lamb or Chicken Curry   (Serves 4)

4 Tbsps. margarine
4 onions
1 clove garlic, chopped fine
1 lb. boneless lamb or chicken, cut into bite-sized pieces
1 cup plain yogurt
curry powder (about 4 tsps., or to taste)

Melt the margarine in a fairly heavy saucepan and add the onions and garlic. Cook on low heat until the onions look transparent. Spoon out the onions and garlic onto a side dish.

Add the meat to the pan and brown quickly all over. Place the onions and garlic back into the pan and add the yogurt and curry powder. Cook very slowly for about a half an hour.

Serve with rice cooked according to directions on the package. Or serve with chapaties from an Indian grocery store. When serving the curry dish, add small side dishes of condiments. Examples are chutney (spiced fruit), raisins, almonds, peanuts, shredded coconut, or chopped egg.

CLOTHING IN INDIA AND AMERICA

Most Americans are familiar with the Indian *sari,* a beautiful native costume. The majority of Indian women wrap themselves in the long piece of cotton or silk cloth that makes up the sari. Some saris have borders made of gold thread. But even the simplest sari has a beautiful color or pattern. In northern India, women often wear a long shirt over loose pants. They also wear a veil. Jewelry is often an important part of a woman's costume. And throughout India, many women place a red or black dot in the middle of their forehead. Called a *bindi,* this dot is a mark of beauty.

In some regions, men too wrap themselves in a long piece of cloth. Many turn the cloth into a kind of loose pants called a *dhoti.* In the North, men wear long, snug coats over pants. Many Indian men also wear turbans. But in the cities, some Indians, especially men, wear Western clothes.

Blending East and West   In the United States, Asian Indians are likely to wear clothes that blend the two cultures. Men often wear Western-style clothing. Sikhs, however, maintain their turbans. Some Asian Indian women usually keep to the traditional sari. But in colder climates, a silk sari will be topped by a winter coat, and warm boots will replace sandals. Even women who adopt Western dress will wear the sari to Indian ceremonies and festivals. A few men, too, will return to Indian dress on special occasions.

The children of Asian Indian immigrants almost always wear Western-style clothing. Like their mothers, older girls are likely to have special saris for religious ceremonies and festivals.

This Sikh family (top right) is dressed in traditional clothing and turbans. The Hindu woman holding her child (bottom right) is dressed in a sari.

AMERICANS TURN TO THE EAST

Americans, too, have blended Western and Eastern cultures. During the 1960s, many young people looked to Eastern religions and culture as a way of improving their lives. Thousands came to believe that Eastern practices such as yoga and transcendental meditation could help cure social as well as personal problems. Psychologists began to look at Eastern practices as a way to help people relieve stress.

During this time, a number of Americans traveled to India to find *gurus*. These are masters who could teach them how to reach a state of spiritual understanding called enlightenment.

Yoga   Yoga is an ancient form of mental and physical exercise. It is made up of exercises for breathing, relaxation, stretching, and concentration. The aim of these exercises is to help people gain better physical and emotional health. Unlike other kinds of exercise, yoga is performed slowly. Greater strength and flexibility are developed gently as time goes on.

Yoga exercises have helped people with various ailments. Studies report, for example, that yoga is the most successful treatment for back pain. Yoga can also help people suffering from

The lotus position, one of many yoga exercises, can take years to achieve.

arthritis become more flexible. And unlike medications or more strenuous forms of exercise, it has no side effects.

In yoga, the mind as well as the body is exercised. Yoga teaches people how to reduce stress by clearing their mind of thoughts. People who succeed report a great feeling of peace. When they are finished with their exercise, they feel refreshed and are calm.

Transcendental Meditation (TM) In 1959 a guru named the Maharishi Mahesh Yogi first brought TM to the United States. TM is aimed at making people more relaxed and creative.

Practicing TM requires two 20-minute sessions a day. During each session, the person sits in a comfortable position and silently repeats a phrase called a *mantra*. A mantra is a pleasant sound with no meaning that is said to soothe the brain with its vibrations. Each person has his or her own mantra. As the session goes on, the mind empties of thought and the person reaches a peaceful state.

Scientists have found that when people practice TM, their blood pressure, breathing, and heart rates drop. At the same time, their alpha waves increase. Alpha waves are brain waves that show a relaxed state of mind. During TM, many people enter a state of rest that is deeper than sleep. When they finish, they feel calm and energetic. People who practice TM regularly report that they accomplish more at work and sleep better at night.

TM may have great effects on a person's health by reducing stress, which doctors now know can lead to serious illness. One recent study divided the elderly patients in a nursing home into three groups. One group practiced TM. Another group used another relaxation technique. The third group did neither. Doctors found that the patients in the TM group showed the greatest improvement in memory and the biggest drop in blood pressure. They also lived longer than the other groups.

ASIAN INDIANS TODAY: A SUCCESS STORY

During the ninety years since the first Asian Indians arrived here, much has happened. For years, many laws and practices in the United States kept them down, kept them apart, and kept them out. But the gradual easing of restrictions toward all groups of immigrants has had happy results for Asian Indians in particular. Their communities grow larger and stronger as their success in different areas persuades others to make the journey from India to the New World.

Numbers tell some of the story of Asian Indians in the United States. Estimates vary, but almost 700,000 Asian Indians now make their homes here. Before 1970, there were

Many Asian Indians own businesses in America.

Many Asian Indians have opened clothing stores in the United States. They work hard to make their stores into successes.

only about 75,000. And before Public Law 483 in 1946, there were just a few thousand. Since Asian Indians living here have a very low birth rate, most of the increase comes from immigration. Asian Indians now make up more than 10 percent of all Asian Americans.

Highest Income Group Other numbers tell more about the success of Asian Indians in America. Fewer than 5 percent live below the poverty line, and fewer receive public assistance than almost any other group of Americans. Asian Indians are far more likely to be found at the upper end of the income scale.

Many Asian Indians in this country save from 20 to 40 percent of their incomes. By any standard, that is a remarkable accomplishment. The national average for all people is 10 percent. What are they saving for? Their goals are part of the

American dream. They want to buy their own businesses. They want to buy their own homes. Many, even those in lower income groups, are managing to do what they set out to do. In some areas, half of the Asian Indians own their own homes.

In Business One reason for the high income of Asian Indians is that many arrived with some money and skills. They also have a great capacity for hard work. Those who start their own shops or farms think nothing of putting in workdays of fourteen hours and more. They even deliberately enter fields that demand long hours, such as motel work.

To win customers, Indian shop owners may offer extra services. One woman who started her own Indian clothing store in New Jersey did free alterations on even the least expensive garments. She became so successful that she has moved her shop into larger quarters three times.

Another reason for success in business is the close-knit Indian family. Parents, children, and other relatives often pitch in to help a new business get off the ground.

Asian Indians in the services, sciences, and professions are well regarded for similar reasons. They work hard in areas such as medicine, which may also demand long hours.

At School Asian Indians also save to educate their children. And even parents who themselves have little education are sending their children to college. The 1980 census showed that 52 percent of adult Asian Indians were college graduates. This compared to 35 percent of all adult Asian Americans. Clearly Asian Indians see education as a way for their children to improve their lives and perhaps do better than their parents.

From grade school through college, Asian Indians tend to succeed in school. Those who come here as college students do remarkably well. More than three out of four earn above-average grades in their courses. One reason for their outstanding performance is their fluency in English.

Another reason is desire. Indian students—of all ages—want to do well. They learn from their parents that education opens the door to opportunity. They want to walk through that door. As a result, Asian Indian high school and college students often win awards and honors.

Students who do not speak English when they arrive here have a harder time. But most work hard to master English and succeed in their studies. They too look at education as the way to success.

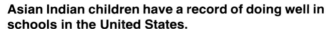

Asian Indian children have a record of doing well in schools in the United States.

DISCRIMINATION

Despite these gains, some Asian Indians report discrimination in jobs and housing. Children and teenagers in particular may have difficulties with their Indian appearance and ways. In one California school, for example, Indian students have been teased and sometimes attacked by other students. They have been laughed at for their hair, their clothing, and the foods they eat. Yet they cling to their Indian traditions.

"Dotbusters"   More serious attacks upon Asian Indians have occurred from the East Coast to the West Coast. Jersey City, New Jersey, home to a community of 10,000 Asian Indians, has reported the worst outbreak. For several years during the mid-1980s, gangs of white, black, and Hispanic youths taunted Asian Indians. In 1987, an Indian man was beaten to death by one of the gangs. At the same time, a letter was published in the *Jersey Journal* saying that ". . . we will go to any extreme to get Indians to move out of Jersey City. If I am walking down the street and I see a Hindu and the setting is right, I will just hit him or her. We plan some of our extreme attacks, such as breaking windows—we use the phone book and look up the name Patel." It was signed "The Dotbusters." Their name comes from the dot that many Indian women wear in the middle of the forehead.

Why?   Asian Indians' different ways and looks are probably one reason for the attacks. But being successful is another, according to Anthony Cucci, mayor of Jersey City at the time. He saw the attacks as signs of jealousy toward a community of people who are often wealthier than those around them. Mayor Cucci noted that Asian Indians are extremely hard workers who have earned their way. Both Mayor Cucci and the then governor of New Jersey, Thomas Kean, praised the Indian community and deplored the racial attacks.

ASIAN INDIANS ARE MAKING THEIR CONTRIBUTION

It is important to remember that the terrible incidents just described are rare. The great majority of Asian Indians still enjoy the United States as a land of opportunity. They have contributed to this country as workers in many different fields. The farmers in the rich valleys of California, the doctors in the large hospitals of the East and Midwest, and the students learning in classrooms throughout the country have all become part of the American scene.

Their unique customs and beliefs are now serving to enrich the culture of this country. Most Americans see the Asian Indians who live here as valuable members of our diverse country, fellow citizens and fellow Americans. They recognize that accepting and learning about these differences makes all our lives fuller. Asian Indians are indeed making their contribution.

Asian Indians celebrate their Indian heritage in this parade float.

SOURCES

Chandrasekhar, C. *From India to America*. La Jolla, Cal.: Population Review, 1982.

Daniels, Roger. *History of Indian Immigration to the United States*. New York: The Asia Society, 1989.

Kitano, Harry H. L., and Roger Daniels. *Asian Americans*. Englewood Cliffs, N.J.: Prentice Hall, 1988.

Saran, Paratma. *The Asian Indian Experience in the United States*. Cambridge, Mass.: Schenkman, 1985.

Takaki, Ronald. *Strangers from a Different Shore*. Boston: Little, Brown, 1989.

Thernstrom, Stephan, ed. *Harvard Encyclopedia of American Ethnic Groups*. Cambridge, Mass.: Harvard University Press, 1980.

INDEX

64